LOSING A TOOTH

by Nicole A. Mansfield

PEBBLE
a capstone imprint

Published by Pebble, an imprint of Capstone
1710 Roe Crest Drive, North Mankato, Minnesota 56003
capstonepub.com

Copyright © 2023 by Capstone. All rights reserved. No part of this publication may be reproduced in whole or in part, or stored in a retrieval system, or transmitted in any form or by any means, electronic, mechanical, photocopying, recording, or otherwise, without written permission of the publisher.

Library of Congress Cataloging-in-Publication Data
Names: Mansfield, Nicole A., author. Title: Losing a tooth / by Nicole A. Mansfield.
Description: North Mankato, Minnesota : Pebble, an imprint of Capstone, [2023] | Series: My teeth | Includes bibliographical references and index. | Audience: Ages 5-8 | Audience: Grades K-1 | Summary: "Uh-oh! You've got a loose tooth! Don't worry. Losing a tooth is a normal process our body goes through. What do you do? Find out in this easy-to-read Pebble Emerge book. With simple text and color photos, young readers will learn all about their teeth"-- Provided by publisher.
Identifiers: LCCN 2022029306 (print) | LCCN 2022029307 (ebook) |
   ISBN 9780756570835 (hardcover) | ISBN 9780756571191 (paperback) |
   ISBN 9780756570934 (ebook PDF) | ISBN 9780756571214 (kindle edition)
Subjects: LCSH: Deciduous teeth--Juvenile literature. | Tooth loss--Juvenile literature.
Classification: LCC QP88.6 .M365 2023 (print) | LCC QP88.6 (ebook) | DDC 612.3/11--dc23/eng/20220720
LC record available at https://lccn.loc.gov/2022029306
LC ebook record available at https://lccn.loc.gov/2022029307

Editorial Credits
Editor: Ericka Smith; Designer: Sarah Bennett; Media Researcher: Svetlana Zhurkin; Production Specialist: Katy LaVigne

Consultant Credits
Patricia V. Hermanson, DMD, MS

Image Credits
Getty Images: Debra L. Tuttle, 5, EyeEm/Adedapo Adegboyega, 18, FatCamera, 9, Layland Masuda, 8, MarsYu, 11, Peter Dazeley, 12, Vudhikul Ocharoen, 17; Shutterstock: asiandelight, 15, Designifty, 1 (smiling tooth), fizkes, 7, Nina Buday, cover, Perfectorius, cover (design elements), poonsap, 19, Rvector (background), 3, 22–23, 24, Savicic, 4, sruilk, 14, Yaroslav Mishin, 19, Zhanna Markina (background), cover, back cover, and throughout, 13; Svetlana Zhurkin: 20

All internet sites appearing in back matter were available and accurate when this book was sent to press.

Printed in the United States   5555

Table of Contents

How Losing a Tooth Begins 4

Your Teeth and Gums 6

How It All Works 10

My Lost Tooth Journal 20

Glossary 22

Read More 23

Internet Sites 23

Index 24

About the Author 24

Words in **bold** are in the glossary.

How Losing a Tooth Begins

You've probably eaten an apple many times. When you bite down, you expect your teeth to stay put. One day you might feel a tooth move. You have a loose tooth!

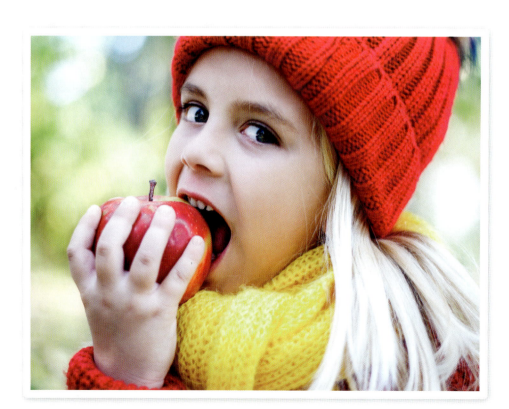

Having a loose tooth is normal for a kid. It won't be long before it falls out. But don't worry! A new tooth will replace it.

Your Teeth and Gums

Babies are born with two sets of teeth. Both hide under the baby's **gums**, inside the **jaw**. They wait there until it's time to come out. This process is called **eruption**.

As babies grow, their first teeth start to erupt. These **primary teeth** usually start to erupt at about six months old. Primary teeth are small.

As kids grow bigger, they need bigger teeth to match! So they start to lose their primary teeth.

This makes room for their second set. They are **permanent teeth**. Kids will have these teeth for the rest of their lives.

How It All Works

At around age six, kids start to lose their primary teeth. And their permanent teeth start to erupt. This process happens slowly. It takes years.

The process usually ends at about age twelve. But the time it takes is different for every kid.

Most kids lose their front teeth first.
Molars usually fall out last. They are bigger teeth. They are in the back of your mouth.

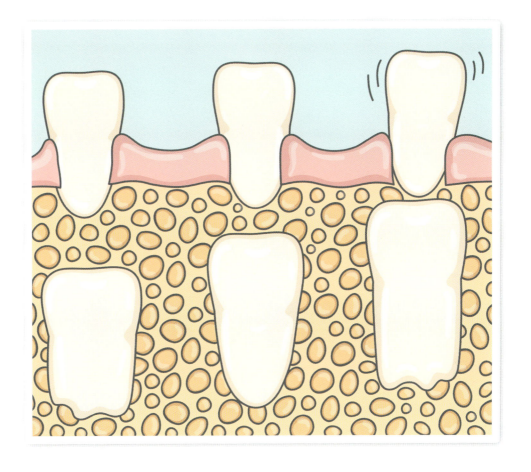

When it's time to lose a tooth, the permanent tooth will start to push on the primary tooth. The primary tooth's **root** begins to melt away. It becomes loose.

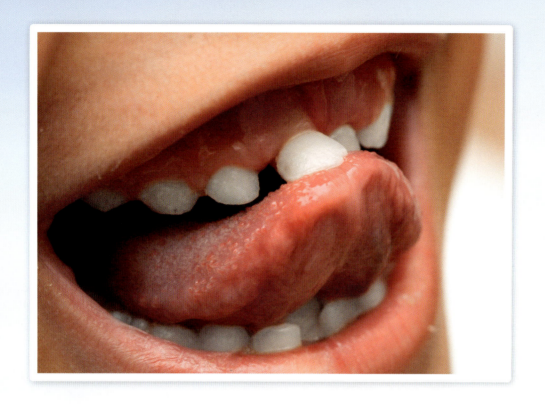

You may want to wiggle a loose tooth. It's okay to wiggle it gently. You can try to wiggle it with your tongue.

Sometimes having a loose tooth is uncomfortable. Eating might be hard. Speaking might be hard too.

If your loose tooth is uncomfortable, you can help it come out. Get a piece of tissue. Use it to grab the loose tooth. Be gentle. Then, squeeze the tooth at the base. Don't yank or pull on your tooth. Forcing a tooth out can harm your gums.

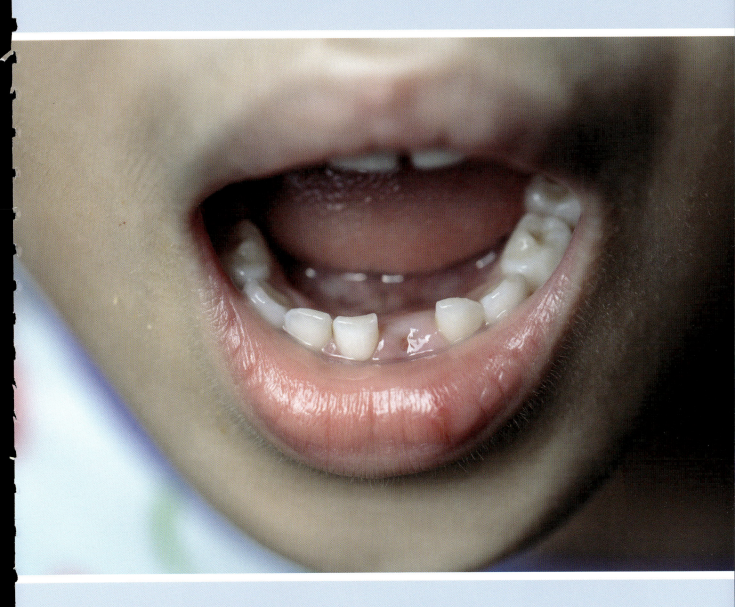

It's normal to lose a tooth. In fact, losing your teeth is an exciting part of growing up!

Now you know what will happen. So there's no need to be afraid when you feel a loose tooth in your mouth. Your body will take care of it!

My Lost Tooth Journal

You've learned a lot about losing a tooth. Try making a journal you can use to express your thoughts and feelings as you lose your primary teeth.

What You Need

- 1 piece of construction paper
- markers, crayons, or colored pencils
- 5 sheets of plain white or lined paper
- stapler
- pencil

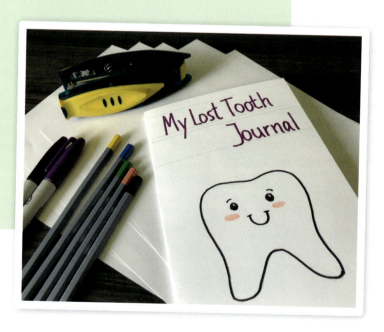

What You Do

1. Fold your piece of construction paper in half from left to right.

2. At the top of your paper, use markers, crayons, or colored pencils to write "My Lost Tooth Journal."

3. Next, draw a picture on the front of your journal. It should show something important about teeth. This will be your cover.

4. Neatly stack your 5 sheets of paper. Then, fold them in half from left to right.

5. Place the paper inside of your cover. Then, staple them along the folded edge.

6. On the first page, write or draw as much information as you can about losing a tooth.

Use the rest of the blank pages to write down the dates when you lose your teeth. Then, write or draw to show your thoughts and feelings about losing each tooth. As you fill your journal, share it with a friend!

Glossary

eruption (ih-RUHP-shuhn)—the act of breaking through

gum (GUHM)—the firm flesh around the base of a person's tooth

jaw (JAW)—the part of the skull that supports the mouth

molar (MOH-lur)—a wide tooth that people use to chew food; molars are in the back of the mouth

permanent teeth (PUR-muh-nuhnt TEETH)—a person's second set of teeth; the teeth you have as an adult

primary teeth (PRYE-mair-ee TEETH)—a person's first set of teeth

root (ROOT)—the part of the tooth that holds it in the mouth

Read More

Mansfield, Nicole A. *All About Teeth*. North Mankato, MN: Capstone, 2023.

Turner, Aziyah. *The Loose Tooth*. Jeffersonville, IN: BK Royston, 2021.

Willems, Mo. *I Lost My Tooth*. New York: Hyperion Books for Children, 2018.

Internet Sites

The Conversation: Curious Kids: Why Do We Lose Our Baby Teeth?
theconversation.com/curious-kids-why-do-we-lose-our-baby-teeth-111911

YouTube: How Teeth Grow (National Institutes of Health)
youtube.com/watch?v=d_CUKWZ1r94

YouTube: Why Do We Have Baby Teeth? (SciShow Kids)
youtube.com/watch?v=3Gy_gts86jM

Index

eruption, 6, 10

gums, 6, 16

jaws, 6

molars, 12

permanent teeth, 9, 10, 13

primary teeth, 6, 8, 10, 13

roots, 13

About the Author

Nicole A. Mansfield dedicates all of her children's books to her own three children—Victorious, Justine, and Zion. She lives in Georgia and is passionate about singing at her church. Nicole loves to take long walks with her kids and her active-duty military husband of 19 years.